BERKLEE BASIC GUITAR

WILLIAM LEAVITT

T0210260

PHASE 2

Berklee Press

Director: Dave Kusek
Managing Editor: Debbie Cavalier
Marketing Manager: Ola Frank
Sr. Writer/Editor: Jonathan Feist

ISBN 978-0-7935-5526-0

1140 Boylston Street
Boston, MA 02215-3693 USA
(617) 747-2146

Visit Berklee Press Online at
www.berkleepress.com

DISTRIBUTED BY

HAL•LEONARD®
CORPORATION
7777 W. BLUEMOUND RD. P.O. BOX 13819
MILWAUKEE, WISCONSIN 53213

Visit Hal Leonard Online at
www.halleonard.com

Introduction

This book is a continuation of the study begun in Phase I. Once again, the intention is to provide FUN WHILE LEARNING still more about the guitar and the language of music. However, since this is Phase II, the material will be found to be somewhat more difficult to master than in your previous lessons, and will require diligent practice and regular review.

Special two, three, four and five part arrangements are included, which are designed to provide fun through musically interesting material for class instruction, guitar clubs and student recitals. All arrangements of three or more parts are playable as duets and therefore Phase II can be successfully used for individual instruction as well as group situations.

As before, I wish you good luck, and sincerely hope you enjoy these studies...

Wm. G. Leavitt

William G. Leavitt

Maidens Wish

Chopin

SIXTEENTH NOTES

Sixteenth notes receive half the time value of eighth notes...
So sixteenth notes are played twice as fast as eighths.

Study

Joy to the World

($\frac{2}{4}$ Time = 2 beats per measure, ♩ = 1 beat)

Handel

Chorale #38

(For duet use 1st and 4th parts)

J.S. Bach

(Observe key signature)

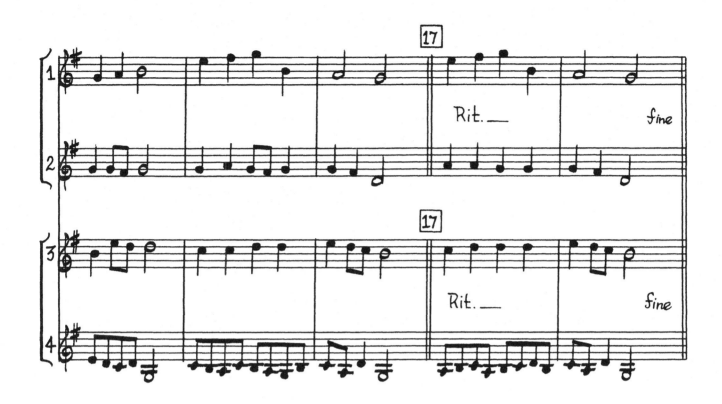

CHORD STUDY IN C

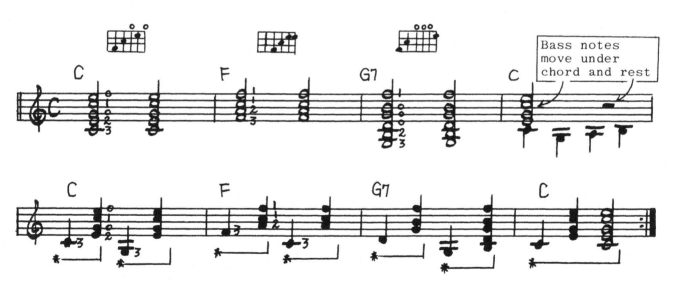

Bass notes move under chord and rest

* With this type of Bass-Chord pattern, it is usually desirable to hold the bass note and/or let it ring as you strum the chord.

CHROMATICS   (This study is important... practice thoroughly.)

THE CHROMATIC SCALE   HAS 12 NOTES, EACH A HALF STEP APART.

Chromatic Scale starting on C

Chromatic Scale starting on G

ASSIGNMENTS   ...Observing time signature, draw in bar lines...play.

Glow Worm

Count On Me

W.G.L.

Included in the following study, are two new musical terms... D.C. (Da Capo) means to play again from the beginning... al coda means to skip to the coda ⊕

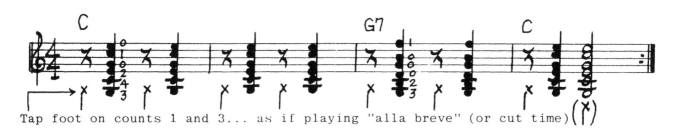

Tap foot on counts 1 and 3... as if playing "alla breve" (or cut time)

Boom-Chick
(RHYTHM GUITAR STUDY)

W.G.L.

(Strum preceding chord again)

CHORD STUDY IN G

*(Hold the bass notes and/or let them ring as you strum the chords.)

The Happy Farmer

R. Schumann

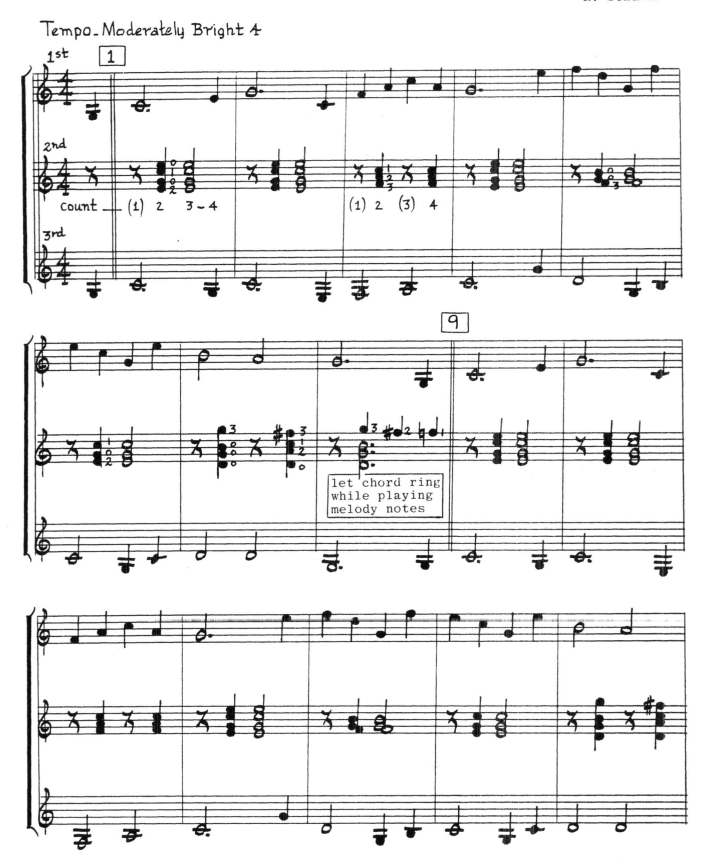

Note: All arrangements (except Chorales) are playable as duets with 1st and
2nd (or lead and 1st rhythm) parts. The student, however, should
practice all parts of each arrangement.

My Wild Irish Rose

Olcott

12

Polly Wolly Doodle Rock

(Arranged to be played with 2, 3, 4 or 5 separate parts)

*(These are rehearsal letters... to aid in group practice of certain sections of this arrangement.)

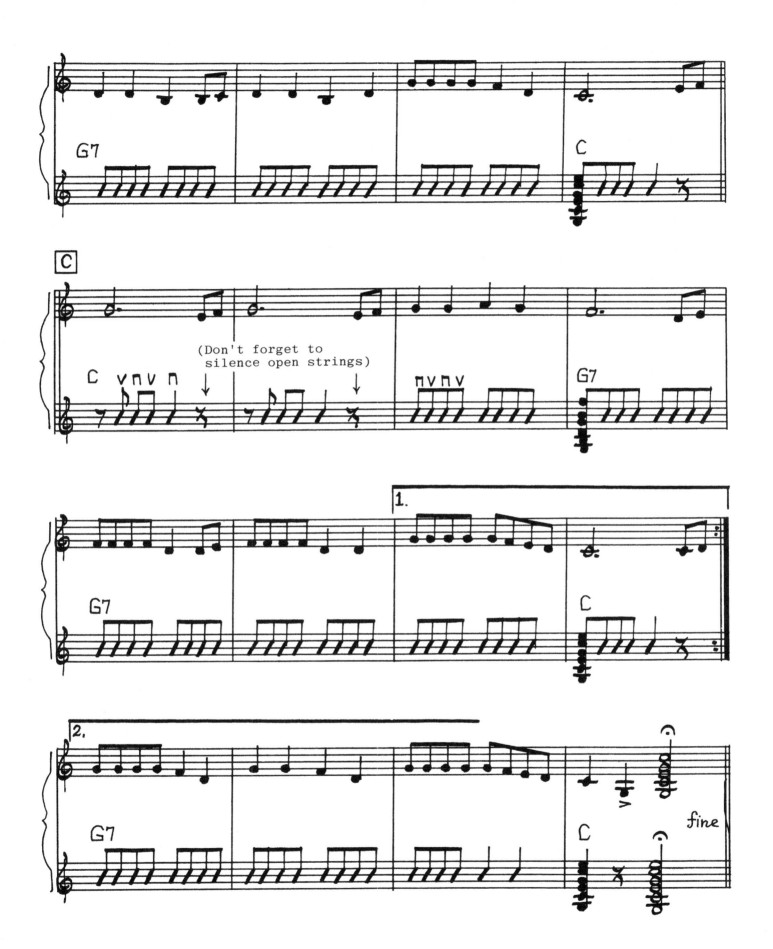

(Don't forget to
silence open strings)

Polly Wolly Doodle Rock

(OPTIONAL PARTS)

Not too fast ♩ = 144

* This "BASS PART" is to be played on a regular guitar with the MUFFLED EFFECT. This is achieved by laying the outer edge of the right hand palm lightly ON the strings ALONG the top of the bridge as you pick.

** Rhythm guitar parts do not always have the chord voicings written out. Often only the chord symbols and rhythms are given... The chord voicings are left to the discretion of the player.

THE F MAJOR SCALE ...(All B's are flatted)

Remember the B is flatted in the Key Signature

Scale Study

1st

2nd

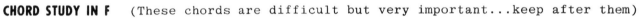

CHORD STUDY IN F   (These chords are difficult but very important...keep after them)

F

Keep fingers pressed down

Bb

C7

Bb   C7   F

F

✱

Bb

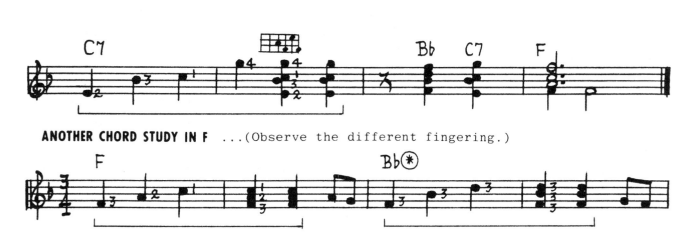

ANOTHER CHORD STUDY IN F ...(Observe the different fingering.)

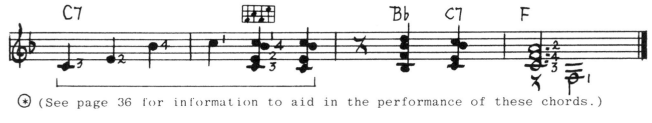

⊛ (See page 36 for information to aid in the performance of these chords.)

Catch Me

W.G.L.

Chorale # 26

(For duet use 1st and 4th parts)

J.S. Bach

Lirpa-Lee Melody

W.G.L.

(Play Bass part on regular guitar using the "muffled effect".)

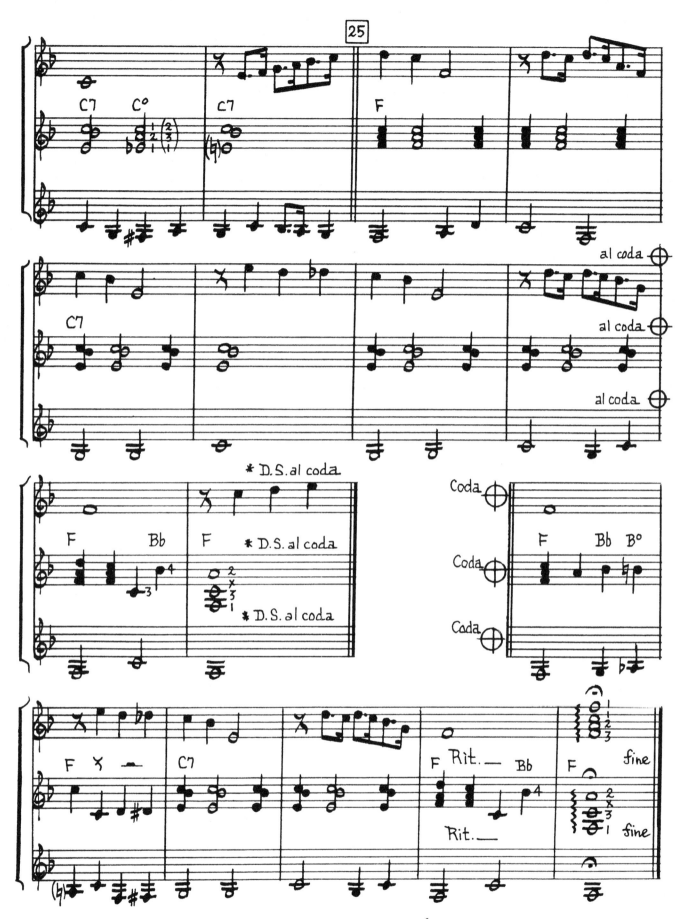

Big Rock Candy Mountain

(Folk Song)

* Be sure to mute 6th string in these chord voicings... See Pg. 42 PHASE I

At a slow tempo, six-eight time is counted 1-2-3-4-5-6 with each eighth note receiving one full beat. At a faster speed, the measure is divided in half and counted "in two" (with the "in between" beats being felt instead of actually counted).

Study

ASSIGNMENT ...Observing time signature, draw in bar lines... play.

Two for Six Eight

W.G.L.

Chop Sticks

AN INTRODUCTION TO MINOR SCALES

Each Major Key has a Relative Minor Key. They are related because the Key Signature is the same.

1. The 6th note of a major scale is the name of it's relative minor scale.
2. On the staff, the 6th note of a major scale is located an interval of a 3rd below the Tonic (or 1st) note of that scale... (A line below a note on a line, or a space below a note on a space).

When discussing C Major, C is the principal or Tonic note... When discussing A Minor, the note A is the Tonic or 1st note.

You will observe below that there are several types of minor scales.

C Major Scale

A Natural Minor Scale (has exactly the same notes as C Major, but starts on A)

A Harmonic Minor Scale (has the 7th note of the minor scale raised 1/2 step)

Note: In addition to the two presented above, there are still other types of minor scales... Traditional Melodic Minor, Real Melodic Minor and Mixed Minor. It is not necessary to be concerned with them at this time.

CHORD STUDY IN A (HARMONIC) MINOR

More Bach Talk

(Excerpt from 2 part Invention No. 4)

J.S. Bach

*special fingering necessary
for smooth, fast playing

AND ANOTHER CHORD STUDY IN F

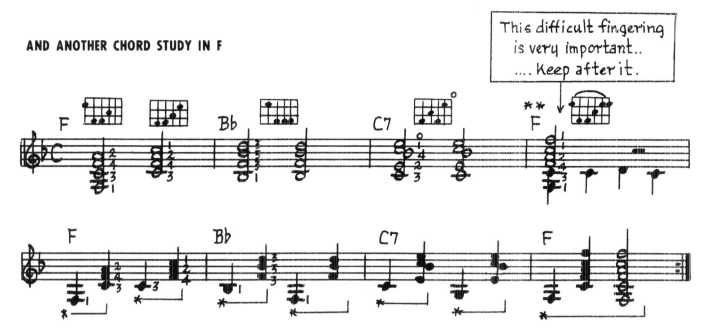

This difficult fingering is very important.. ....keep after it.

** 1st finger pressed across all strings is called a "Grand Barre"

(See page 36 for info to aid in performance of some of the preceding chords)

THE TRIPLET

Count 1 2 & ah 3 4
(2 trip-let)

1 2 & ah 3 4 & ah
(2 trip-let) (4 trip-let)

When The Saints Go Marchin' In

(Arranged to be played with 2, 3, 4 or 5 separate parts)

* Avoid striking open bottom string, or mute by lightly touching with
  tip of 3rd finger.

When The Saints Go Marchin' In

(OPTIONAL PARTS)

* This Bass part is to be played on a regular guitar with the "muffled effect".

ABOUT BARRE (and Partial Barre) CHORDS

When the 1st or 3rd fingers are required to press down more than one string at a time to form a chord, the following information is important...

1. Place the 1st finger almost directly ON the fret needed, and as you apply pressure roll the 1st finger toward the next lower fret (toward the nut).

2. Place the 3rd finger a little further back from the fret needed, and as you apply pressure roll the 3rd finger toward the fret (toward the body).

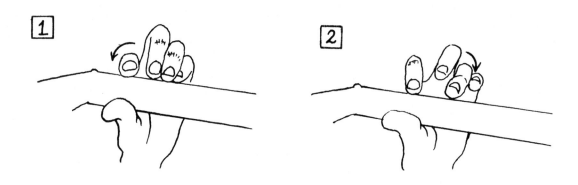

Since there is less flesh on the side of the fingers, and because rolling the fingers as described above causes a leverage situation between the thumb and the 1st or 3rd finger, these chords sound clearer almost immediately.

G MAJOR AND E MINOR SCALES

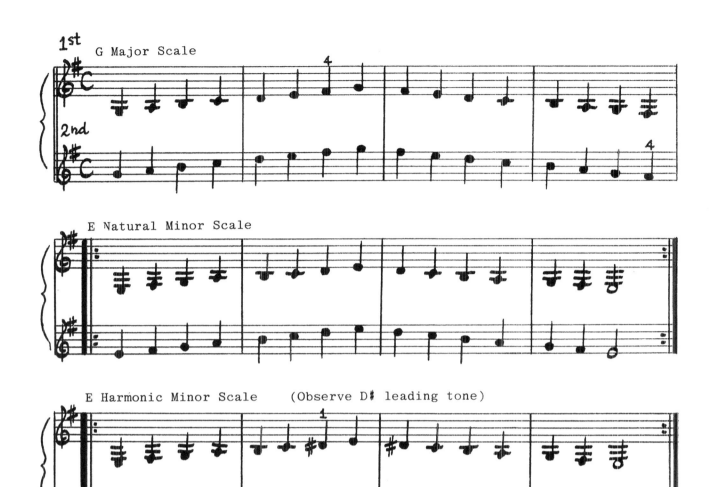

CHORD STUDY IN E (HARMONIC) MINOR

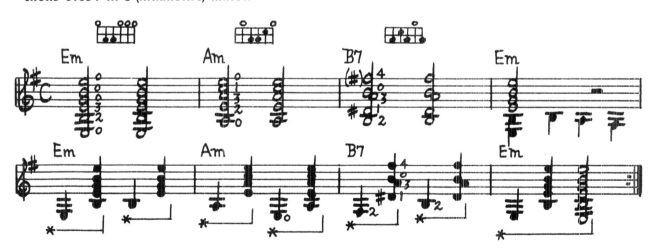

A Short Sad Song

Remember the
accent mark (>)
means to
strike more
sharply.

Also: The
change of
key in this
arrangement
is called a
"Modulatio⌐

Jeanie With the Light Brown Hair

S. Foster

41

F MAJOR AND D MINOR SCALES

F Major

D Natural Minor

D Harmonic Minor

CHORD STUDY IN D (HARMONIC) MINOR

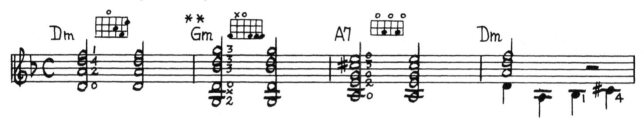

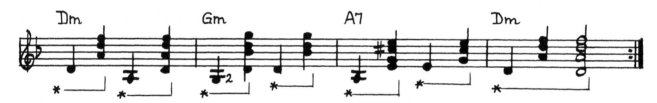

**(Be careful to mute 5th string with this Gmin chord.)

A Very Minor Etude

W.G.L.

(Observe the various fingerings used for the A7 chord)

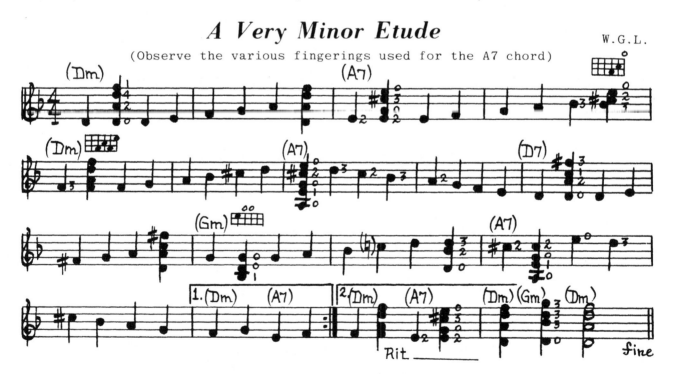

Short On Bread

(This is a very important study of syncopated rhythms... learn them well.)

Merry Old Smobile

45

Bb MAJOR AND G MINOR SCALES
(All B's and E's are flatted)

CHORD STUDY IN Bb

CHORD STUDY IN G (HARMONIC) MINOR

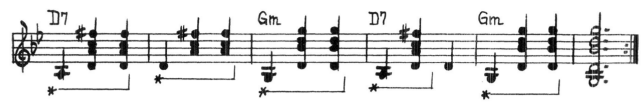

Catch Me Again

W.G.L.

Softshoe Shuffle

W.G.L.

Lead Guitar

Hava Nagila

Tempo In 2

(Tacet.. 4 measures)

An orchestral presentation has been used for this arrangement using
separate parts, so that the student will become accustomed to reading
his part without the aid of seeing the others to help him keep his place.

Hava Nagila

Bass Part (To be played on a regular guitar with the muffled effect.)

D MAJOR AND B MINOR SCALES
(All F's and C's are sharped)

CHORD STUDY IN D

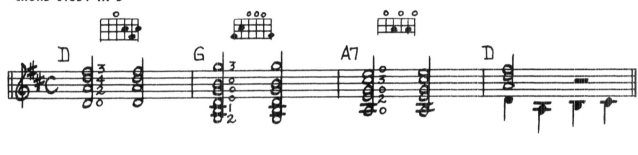

Note: Chord studies in certain keys will not be presented, as some of the voicings in the 1st position are too weak for rhythm accompaniment. Movable chord forms (to be presented in PHASE III) are needed for them.

Another Very Minor Etude

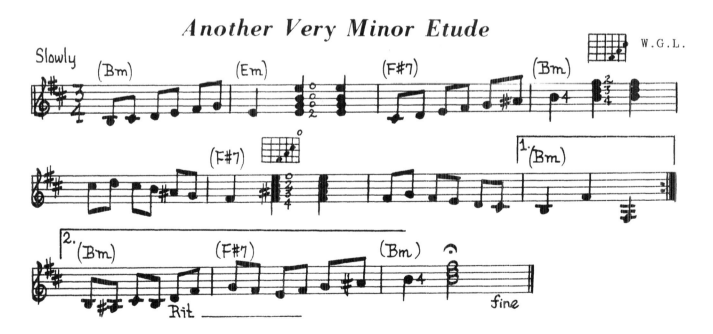

La Paloma

S. Yradier

55

Fifty Rocks

W.G.L.

(Be careful of the syncopation in melody and bass parts)

(Play Bass part with muffled effect)

A MAJOR AND F# MINOR SCALES

(All F's, C's and G's are sharped)

CHORD STUDY IN A

* This reminder to keep the bass notes ringing, will not be found on other guitar literature... It will be up to you to apply this technique when appropriate.

A Very Very Minor Etude

W.G.L.

Spanish March

W.G.L.

59

Eb MAJOR AND C MINOR SCALES

(All B's, E's and A's flatted in the signature)

Don't Forget To Count On Me

W.G.L.

A Not So Minor Etude

W.G.L.

THEORY

(Observe the pattern on the fingerboard.)

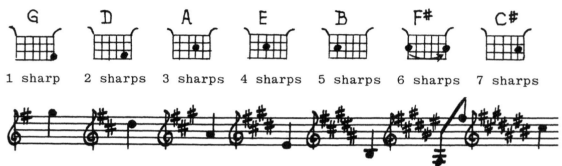

The next letter name above the last sharp in the signature is the name of the major key.

Observe that in this evolution of sharp keys, the new sharp that is added is always the note preceding the letter name of the new key. (This is called the "leading tone".)

EVOLUTION OF MAJOR KEYS THAT CONTAIN FLATS

(Observe the pattern on the fingerboard.)

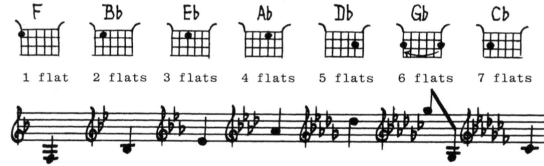

You must memorize the key signature of F major. To determine the name of all other major keys that contain flats, merely use the letter name of the next to the last flat in the signature.

Observe that in this evolution of flat keys, the new flat that is added is always the name of the next key in the sequence.

TABLE OF MAJOR AND RELATIVE MINOR KEYS

MAJOR KEYS	C	C#	Db	D	Eb	E	F	F#	Gb	G	Ab	A	Bb	B	C
MINOR KEYS	Am		Bbm	Bm	Cm	C#m	Dm		Ebm	Em	Fm	F#m	Gm	G#m	Abm

62